Capillary Action:
Verse in a Light Vein

Other books by David Hedges

Petty Frogs on the Potomac (1997)

The Wild Bunch (1998)

Brother Joe (2000)

Steens Mountain Sunrise: Poems of the Northern Great Basin (2004)

Selected Sonnets (2006)

A Funny Thing Happened on My Way to a Geology Degree (2011)

Prospects of Life After Birth: Memoir in Poetry and Prose (2019)

The Changer (2021)

Trump Über Alles: Rhymes for Trying Times (2022)

The Zigzag Papers ~ or ~ Who Wants Wanda Wasted (2023)

The Death of Democracy (2024)

*Capillary Action:*
*Verse in a Light Vein*

David Hedges

Road's End Press

Capillary Action: Verse in a Light Vein
David Hedges

Copyright © 2025 David Hedges

FIRST EDITION

All rights reserved. No part of this book may be reproduced in any manner without the express written consent of the author or Road's End Press except for excerpts in reviews and articles.

Road's End Press
326 Pearl Street
Oregon City, Oregon 97045

To order copies, visit roadsendpress.com

Cover art and illustrations by Jim Agpalza
Design and author photo by Mary Milner
Layout and typography by Andrew Hedges
Proofreading by Valerie Witte

Library of Congress Control Number: 2025942056

ISBN: 978-1-7366102-8-2

Ebook version available

*I dedicate this book
to María, the love of my life,
my Muse*

Acknowledgements

Able Muse:
"Halftime Show at the Super Bowl"

Calapooya Collage:
"Why We Love Miss America Clothed"; "God Bless the Virgins"; "The Chauffeur's Tale"; "The Moon on the Moss Beneath the Virgin"; "Life Is a Beach"

Encore: Prize Poem Anthology, NFSPS:
"Ballade for the Birthday of Cyrano at the Coffee Time Coffee Shop"; "Aubade: Dialogue at Dawn"

Hellas: A Journal of Poetry and the Humanities:
"The Curious Stares and the Hungry Eyes"

Light Quarterly:
"Dances with Marketeers"; "Bouncing Bareback Baby Boomers"; "Hog Tithe"; "The Poetaster"; "Facts Plucked from a Back-cover Ad"; "Relativity"; "The Texas School Board Tackles Geometry"; "Close But No Cigar"

Light: A Journal of Light Verse:
"Cotswold Flasher Bitten By Dog"; "A Trophy Fit for a King"; "How to Feed the Hungry"; "Oh You!"; "A Fleeting Thought"; "Nothing on Earth"; "Flight of the Iguana"; "Birth Control"; "Can't Win"; "Age Appropriate"

The Lyric:
"A Sunday Drive"; "Little Incubator"; "Hangover"

Trinacria:
"The Bare Breast"; "Specific Gravity"; "Rich People"

Verseweavers: Prize Poem Anthology, Oregon Poetry Association:
"They Laughed When I Sat Down to Play"; "A Guide to the Modern Sonnet"; "The Crosscut in the Crotch"; "The Spartans Versus the Athenians"; "The Darling Buds of Barbara Bush"; "Let's Do Lunch"; "A Good Day to Die"

Table of Contents

Dedication

Acknowledgements

Events & Affairs

- 3   Capillary Action
- 4   "Cotswold Flasher Bitten by Dog"
- 5   The Bare Breast
- 6   Halftime Show at the Super Bowl
- 7   Why We Love Miss America Clothed
- 9   They Laughed When I Sat Down to Play
- 10   Abner Davenport's Dog
- 11   And Now, the News . . .
- 12   Can't Win

Science & Technology

- 15   Close but No Cigar
- 16   No Sooner the Soup Than the Nuts
- 18   Ferocious Bones
- 19   Space and Time Explained
- 20   Jaw Dropping News
- 22   The Stars Our Destination?
- 23   Blue Moon
- 24   Birth Control

Food & Wine

- 27   The Banana Slug Cookbook
- 28   A Time for Worms
- 29   "Let's Do Lunch"
- 30   A Trophy Fit for a King
- 31   Picking Blackberries
- 32   The Darling Buds of Barbara Bush
- 34   Willie's Wine

Gravity & Greed

- 37 Rich People
- 38 The Trickle-up Theory
- 40 How to Feed the Hungry
- 41 The Fifteen Commandments
- 42 Bouncing Bareback Baby Boomers
- 43 The Battle of Mount Narcissus
- 44 In Praise of Billionaires

Literature & Lore

- 47 The Poetaster
- 48 A Guide to the Modern Sonnet
- 49 Ballade for the Birthday of Cyrano at the Coffee Time Coffee Shop
- 50 In Praise of Peter Sellers
- 51 The Crosscut in the Crotch
- 52 The Moon on the Moss Beneath the Virgin
- 54 The Dillowy Danderhonk
- 60 In Pursuit of My Beautiful Muse
- 62 Kick the Can

Love & Lust

- 65 Stagestruck
- 66 Relativity
- 67 Three Limericks with Titles
- 68 Only Mnemosyne Knows
- 69 God Bless the Virgins
- 70 The Curious Stares and the Hungry Eyes
- 71 I'd Rather Sail My Schooner than Have Sex
- 72 Aubade: Dialogue at Dawn
- 74 Bronze Bosom Above Mahogany Inboard Runabout
- 75 Puppy Love
- 76 A Sunday Drive
- 77 Oh You!
- 78 I'm with You

Health & Happiness

- 81 Little Incubator
- 82 'Tis the Season
- 83 Limerick
- 84 Vector Control
- 85 Willow Creek Hot Springs
- 86 Georgine's Abrupt Recovery
- 87 Unreality Show
- 88 Waking Up in Willoughby
- 89 A Fleeting Thought
- 90 Life is a Beach
- 92 Nothing on Earth

Business & Pleasure

- 95 Hog Tithe
- 96 Dances with Marketeers
- 98 Facts Plucked from a Back-cover Ad
- 99 The Chauffeur's Tale
- 100 Good Little Shoppers

Life & Death

- 103 The Gospel of Fred
- 104 Hangover
- 105 Death Came to Me Last Night
- 106 When Audrey Sailed
- 107 The Lonely Glove
- 108 A Good Day to Die
- 109 Just Desserts
- 110 The Chair: Its Merits
- 112 Age Appropriate

War & Peace

115 Flight of the Iguana
116 The Pre-divorce Contract
118 The Spartans Versus the Athenians

Politics & Bureaucracy

121 Airport Insecurity
122 Curbside Complaint
123 "Fort Wayne Scratches Harry Baals"
124 The Texas School Board Tackles Geography

About the Author

About the Artist

About My Muse

Glossary of Terms & Forms

Events & Affairs

Capillary Action
n., the ability to flow in opposition to the force of gravity

Like water rising to the leaves of trees,
I flow in opposition to the force
That drops repentant souls to bended knees,

Besieged by doubts and saddled with remorse,
Weighed down by fears and overwhelmed with guilt.
My lightness springs from some artesian source

And wells profusely. It's the way I'm built—
My glass runs over. Whether bust or boom,
I drive my comic dagger to the hilt.

My levitation started in the womb
When Mom was plied with drugs to hold me in
Until Doc Frisbee came, and in my tomb

I'll still be chuckling at the Mickey Finn,
And how I drifted into this good day
High as a kite, complete with silly grin.

The only bones I pick are those I play
Like rows of rosewood bars on xylophones,
Or strum like banjo strings, or pluck away

At, as I tickle ribs—the funny bones
I double over with my jokes, wry quips
And flagrant puns. Forget the moans and groans—

Yell *Carpe diem!* as you swing your hips
Down streets and avenues, and misbehave
On Amtrak trains and ocean-going ships.

Go forth and multiply your mirth. Be brave—
Aspire to make the grumblers grab their knees
With laughter. Gravity is for the grave.

"Cotswold Flasher Bitten by Dog"

Headline: *BBC News*

Nobody saw the flasher prowling
Cotswold streets like a thief.
"Short and slim," said Sergeant Dowling,
Himself a side of beef.

"According to the victim, bless her,
The bloke had bluey-brown eyes.
Was what she dubbed a crack undresser,
Trousers to his thighs.

"The victim, bless her, carried a terrier.
Growl, and the bloke was bitten.
Most likely, next time he'll be warier."
And that's the news from Great Britain.

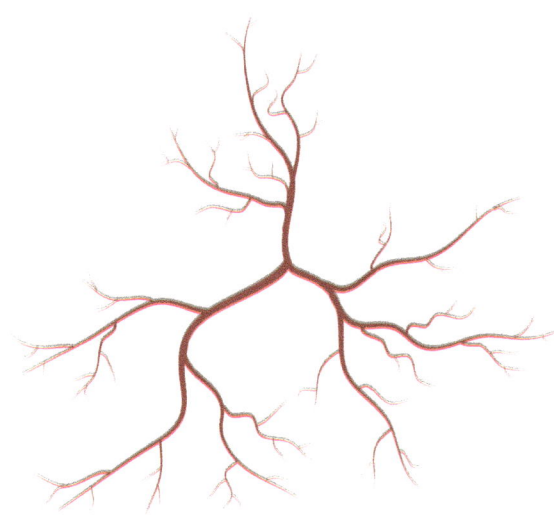

The Bare Breast

Admittedly the day was warm,
Her dress was open to the breeze
On either side. "No risk, no harm,"
My alter ego argued. "Please,

Feel free to gaze, it's not a test
Assessing virtue versus lust.
The view's an ordinary breast,
The looking's something someone must

When seated so." The sky, I knew,
Was out, because a picnic lunch
Was perched upon my knees. To chew,
One needs a level head, and punch

Is difficult to drink while lips
Are poised above the pouring point.
The rationale when someone tips
A cup is rarely to anoint

One's face, but rather, to reduce
One's thirst. And glancing left or right
Is fine at first, but flagrant use
Stirs people in one's line of sight

To move away, or worse, to glare.
My alter ego understood:
"When seated where a breast is bare,
Behold a bust as Rodin would,

Or Renoir, with unvarnished paints,
A nude reclined across the lawn,
Or Michelangelo, whose saints
Parade with next to nothing on."

My artist's eye was primed to draw
The breast a figure sketching class
Undrapes, but when I looked, I saw,
Exposed, a flattened patch of grass.

Halftime Show at the Super Bowl

When Janet Jackson flashed her mamma
The network went ballistic.
Seems bare breasts flop in Alabama
With Foursquare and Baptistic.

What caused the ruckus was a nipple
Which only she possesses—
If we believe the talk-show ripple
And don't bog down in guesses.

It's fine to show the whole enchilada
On the set of Sex in the City
Or in topless bars throughout Nevada.
On the boob tube, it's tough titty.

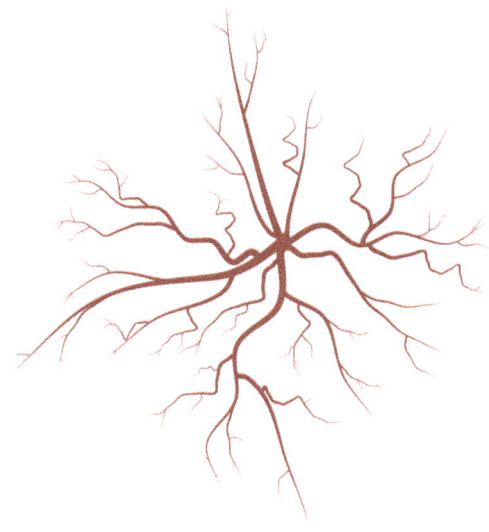

Why We Love Miss America Clothed

"Oh, God, she's nude!"
—Cover of *Penthouse*

A parade of naked
young ladies singing
Opera or Country or Blues
or tap dancing or playing
the violin or accordion
leaves the imagination
stripped of direction.

With no prying eyes
Miss America becomes
just another naked woman
who arouses lust or ire
depending on your frame
of mind and what you feel
needs some protection.

We maintain modesty
around mounds and into
hollows we all know are there
and where the hint puts
more points in a judge's eye
than a bald-faced exposé
of natural perfection.

What titillates comes
from what's withheld
like the ripe plums
just beyond your reach
or the fluttering butterfly
that would for all time
complete your collection.

*They laughed when I sat down to play,
My tails tucked up between my legs.*

They Laughed When I Sat Down to Play

with a wink and a nod to Victor Borge

They laughed when I sat down to play,
My tails tucked up between my legs.
I looked hard at the lewd array
The way a homeless beggar begs,

With soulful and remorseful sighs.
Three thousand gleeful eyeballs popped
At what appeared between my thighs.
To pass the time before it dropped,

I joined the Great Erection Watch.
The fifteen-hundred straitlaced souls
Who brought attention to my crotch
Cracked up like Anasazi bowls,

Their inhibitions unrestrained—
Some ruptured with a mighty roar.
Before their reservoirs were drained,
I turned attention to the score.

Like spiders tidying their strings,
My fingers stroked the ivories.
I watched the tail-end titterings
Through eyes submerged in salty seas.

Primed for rhapsodic intercourse,
The swell recumbent in the trough,
I launched Rachmaninoff with force
Enough to knock their stockings off.

Abner Davenport's Dog

Whenever his late wife's mother calls,
The dog falls dead away on the floor
And stays board-stiff until she bawls
Obscenities on out the door.

Whenever the next-door neighbor knocks
And asks to borrow another tool,
The dog runs in circles, squeals and squawks,
And leaves little puddles of drool.

Whenever a salesman talks himself blue,
The dog gloms on with an awful leer,
Sticking to the poor man's shoe like glue
And filling his eyes with fear.

Whenever the pastor's bride comes to see
How well he's getting along all alone,
And if he's as happy as he can be,
The dog licks her like a bone.

Abner Davenport is prone to treat
Negative reactions to the unrestrained
Doings of his dog on a positive beat:
"I don't understand. He's trained."

And Now, the News...

Headline: *Do it in a microwave oven, save time*

Conserving time is not what matters
When trapped in Tantric lock.
Bread rises, oven heats, one scatters
Mantras—screw the clock.

Headline: *Pastor aghast at first lady sex position*

Why was the pastor there at all?
Why would he give a hoot?
The secret service dropped the ball.
Next time, give him the boot.

Headline: *Child's stool great for use in garden*

See the potty chairs, a group
Between the tulips—rows
Of gleeful tykes assigned to poop
Outdoors without their clothes.

Headline: *Woman off to jail for sex with boys*

I don't think that's the proper way—
Giving her latitude
To teach a boy crime doesn't pay
By earning his gratitude.

Headline: *Mrs. Gandhi Stoned at Rally*

Been there, done that once or twice.
What's a rally for?
It's made rallies really nice
That would've been a bore.

Can't Win

Dame Fortune doesn't know my name.
Claims I have only myself to blame.
Shame she refuses to play my game.
Dame Fame's the same.

Science & Technology

Close but No Cigar

Technology's the source of all our grief.
It strips us to our undies in a light
So harsh our warts pop out in high relief
Like mesas from a desert flat, so bright
Our faculties fly south like geese, a thief
Who picks our pockets as we sleep at night,
Our dreams dictated by the pat belief
That we control our fate through second sight
Greater than Mother Nature's. I'll be brief
In my concluding argument: Not quite.

No Sooner the Soup Than the Nuts

News item: *Four hundred tons of organic "space dust" fall to Earth each year, a small fraction of what fell during Earth's formation.*

The carbon compounds that once crashed to Earth
Like limbs in a windstorm still land like leaves.
Four hundred tons each year, a downright dearth;
Back when, they fell for all the sky was worth.
There's more to matter than the mind conceives.

Earth in those days had heavy metal rock
Bubbling from its molten depths through vents
And cooling like the crust on chicken stock.
Call the world "igneous" and "chockablock."
No wind, no water, thus no sediments.

Into this blast furnace (no lie!) flew ice,
A gift of frozen gas from outer space,
Kamikaze comets whose sacrifice
Wrapped up and ribboned life in paradise
By making Earth a user-friendly place

With an oxygenated atmosphere.
The stuff that landed next contained the cheap
Ingredients of a brew (no, not beer)
Conducive to life on this new frontier—
And here we take a scientific leap:

No sooner the soup than the protoplasts
As clouds commenced to hurl their lightning bolts,
Stirring amoebae to their light repasts,
The shocks enough to cause iconoclasts
To bond. Don't ask how many watts or volts

It took to make the goop electrified.
These single cells soon swam about in schools.
You know the rest: First they learned to divide;
Then, not content with that, they multiplied;
Before long, the brains were packing slide rules.

Next came the age of electronics, where
Everyone promptly forgot how to add
And subtract. In no time, the very air
Was unfit to breathe as the laissez-faire
Conspiracy made bottom lines the fad.

Now people go to zoos to see the few
Remaining beasts, the rhinos and giraffes
Caged in their concrete runs, the marabou
Storks, land tortoises, loons, a caribou
Or two, hyenas sharing their last laughs.

Like a bright, all-too-brief meteorite,
The feast has run its course, the dinner's done.
Smacking our lips with every tender bite,
We've eaten almost everything in sight—
Except assorted nuts, the ones with guns.

Ferocious Bones

A new Cretaceous fossil find in China
Has set the minds of ologists atwitter.
For reference, let's call the reptile Dinah.
As for the mammal who attacked and bit her,
Let's call him Gurgi for the badger Pooh Bear
Knew from Disney flicks as self-effacing.
Fossil folks, with practiced eye and care,
Disentangled skeletons embracing
Not so fondly as abrupt volcanics
Sealed their doom. They'd never seen a struggle
Like Gurgi's spat with Dinah—the dynamics
Smacked of pure-blood wizard versus Muggle . . .
The witty inspiration for this sonnet
Seems somehow to have gotten lost, doggonit!

Space and Time Explained

    Infinity is fairly simple.
      Picture Earth as a tiny pimple
On the gluteus maximus, or bottom,
Of a fleshy hippopotam-
    Us—or, on its cheek, a dimple.

    Eternity is somewhat tricky.
      Here the wicket's rendered sticky
By the schism between thinker
And believer—one's a stinker
    While the other's picky-picky.

    Thinkers revel in extolling
      Time as a stone forever rolling,
A baseball game with no beginning,
Inning after extra inning,
    Balls and strikes galore—or bowling.

    Believers boast a panacea
      Based on the old steadfast idea
Of a strictly codified Creation.
Evolution? *Deviation!*
    Billions of years? *Ave María!*

Jaw Dropping News

Hang on to your hats as a pair of Brits
Drags math and science up to speed.
The Big Bang spattered space with bits

Of matter where once none was—agreed?
Then these two wave their magic wand:
Concentric circles supersede

What's thought to be out there beyond
Creation (nothingness). They think
Echoes ripple the cosmic pond;

Our universe is but a link
In an endless everlasting chain
Reaction—a droplet in the drink.

Such news could cause a body's brain
To atrophy. So what now, God?
Your seven days go down the drain.

Will followers forgive your fraud,
And praise the Brits, and genuflect—
Or take up arms and run roughshod?

How can you hope to resurrect
The monumental bond that binds
Them to your fundamental sect?

Surely they've peeked between the blinds
And seen themselves being fed a crock
While hands massaged their soft behinds

And voices beckoned like a flock
Of geese at dusk on a distant marsh.
Once you excuse yourselves from shock,

Your punishment doesn't seem so harsh—
Doomed to having your mind's-eyes catch
The glint of genius in this farce,

This existential tennis match
Where thinkers and believers rail
And rant at itches they can't scratch.

O Holy Cow, Now Off To Jail,
Do Not Pass Go, Do Not Collect
Two Hundred Bucks, Forget the Grail.

Go forth and wield your intellect.
Buzz through holes in the ball of wax
Until you feel your wires connect.

No one's stalking in your tracks,
Poised to impale you on a spear.
So what's the best advice? Relax.

Release your rage. Let go your fear.
Time and space are tests of wits.
Nothing has changed. Be of good cheer.

The Stars Our Destination?

Professor Stephen Hawking went plumb daft.
He thought humanity should hop to Mars
Aboard a laser-powered nanocraft,
Or even dafter, to the distant stars.

He saw humanity as something worth
Preserving in the scheme of time and space,
But didn't seem to understand that Earth
Is home, and Mother to the human race.

He tried to save us from ourselves, a fate
To which the populace appears blasé.
Among concerns, survival doesn't rate
Up there with Drake and Kendrick's latest fray.

Professor Hawking had a lot of nerve.
By staying here, we spare the universe.
We could, of course, cause climate change to swerve
By shifting from high gear into reverse.

Blue Moon

"Water Ice Detection Delights Lunar Researchers"
—*Space.com*

We knew the Moon was made of green cheese once
And anyone who differed was a dunce.
Then came the knowledge that the cheese was rock
And meteors accounted for the pock-
Marked plains and craters. Ah, but then we struck
A source of drinking water—pure dumb luck.
Last night I heard the water rights were sold
And when I looked, the Moon had turned to gold.

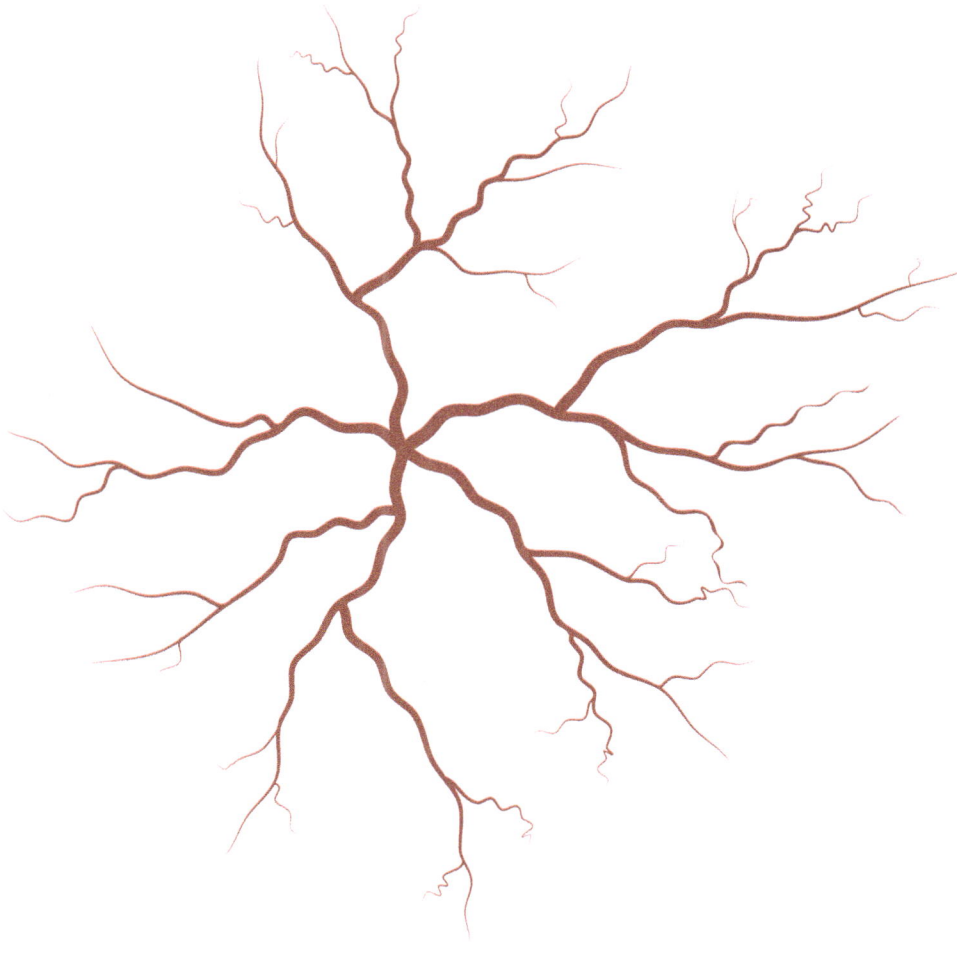

Birth Control

"A Pet Crayfish Can Clone Itself, And It's Spreading Around the World"
—*The Atlantic*

"A single woman might be able to reproduce by herself"
—*NeoLife*

The female crayfish that gives birth
Without a mate, for what it's worth,
Will one day dominate the Earth

By squeezing out the ones that play
By Nature's rules. With sex passé,
This crayfish knows when Mother's Day

Is nigh because she has a choice,
A strong, no longer passive voice,
In when she lays her eggs. Rejoice,

Ye lovers of the human race!
Someday it may be commonplace
To breed without a fond embrace.

The sooner women learn they can
Conceive without a middleman
(Japan is in the research van)

The sooner men will say, "No more
Do we feel free to march to war."
The Women's Diplomatic Corps

Will make a keen appeal for peace,
And armed hostilities will cease.
Communities will charge police

With keeping people safe and sound.
The implications are profound!
(Don't worry, we'll still fool around.)

Food & Wine

The Banana Slug Cookbook

News item: *Climate change and overpopulation will force people to find new food sources.*

News item: *A dung beetle has more protein than a steak. Three crickets have more calcium than a glass of milk.*

Banana slugs have much more appeal
Than bugs such as ants or roaches.
They make for a super-duper meal
Whether one roasts them or poaches.

Fry them up nicely in a pan—
They're crispy as chicken fingers.
Pressure-cook them in a can
So the sealed-in flavor lingers.

Fillet them as you would a fish
If any were left in the deep seas.
Bake them with bark in a casserole dish.
Dry them and eat them as munchies.

Mince or quarter for soup or stew.
Boil as you once did potatoes
Back in the old days when produce grew,
Crops such as beans and tomatoes.

The Banana Slug Cookbook is chockablock
With ways to enjoy gourmet cooking.
Be sure to keep plenty of slugs in a crock
Or you'll waste all your precious time looking.

A Time for Worms

The time has come to speak of worms
In our search for survival information,
For worms rate high on the list in terms
Of what circumvents starvation.

The protein worms deliver ranks
Their bodies better as protein sources
Than chicken and fish and dinner franks
And the meat of cows and horses.

The underground life they follow lends
Unsettling credence to squeamish natures
Who want the bare bones of what offends
Struck from our nomenclatures—

The fact that earthworms make their rounds
In tunnels created by the act of eating
Explains why the mineral count compounds
In whatever worms are excreting—

But worms, ever waiting in the wings,
Shall rise as penultimate earthly creatures
When we have made such a mess of things
We can only watch from the bleachers.

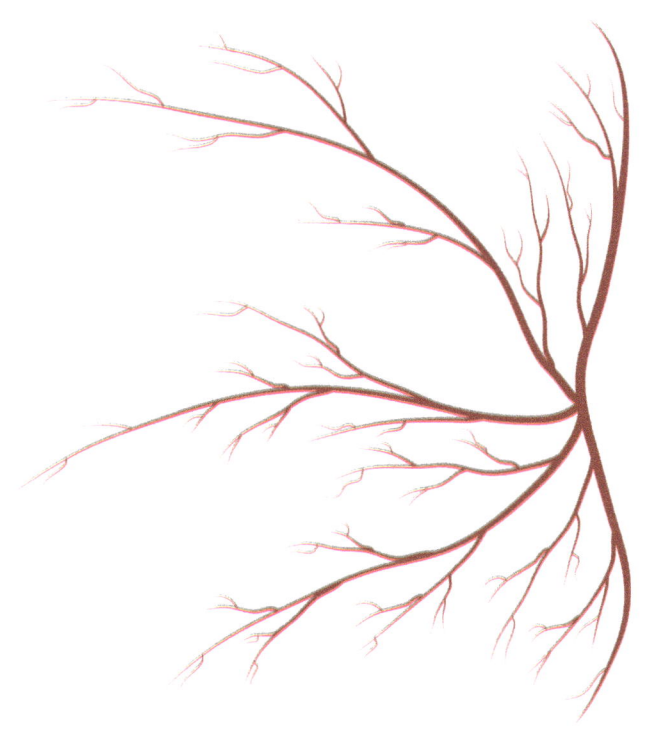

"Let's Do Lunch"

My preppy nephew never wants
To grab a bite. He'd rather *do*
His midday meals at trendy haunts
With chefs trained at Le Cordon Bleu.

He starts off with the soup *du jour.*
His appetizer's *escargot,*
His entrée salmon steak *au beurre,*
And for dessert, the peach *flambeau.*

I scan the menu 'til I'm blind,
Anticipate and agonize,
Hoping in vain that I might find
A bacon burger, shake, and fries.

A Trophy Fit for a King

"South African lions eat 'poacher,'
leaving just his head"
—*BBC News*

A poacher set out with the aim
Of dispatching South African game.
With his Nitro Express,
He was primed for success
And a shoo-in for fortune and fame.

The lions he happened to meet
Were delighted and made haste to eat
Both his lip-smacking haunch
And his succulent paunch,
Not to mention his hands and his feet.

The lions heard voices and fled
Without taking the late poacher's head.
Their intent? To come back,
Mount his head on a plaque
For display on the wall of their den.

Picking Blackberries

Barbs on the undersides of leaves
Rake the back of my picking hand
Like a Zen practitioner tending sand
In a Japanese garden. Double-stitched sleeves
Unzip like riddles my wit conceives,
The Red Sea parting on command,
Cotton uncoupling, strand after strand,
When thorns jimmy in like common thieves.
"Japanese flags," she dubbed the jots
Of toilet paper stuck to my face
Back when I shaved. Now it's my arm
That bleeds rising suns, forget-me-nots
On Oxford-cloth shirts from my button-down days.
How sweet the berries when they're warm.

The Darling Buds of Barbara Bush

Barbara Bush was bound for glory
Before her buds began to rot—
But hold on, that's another story.
She was a plum, an apricot,

Before her buds began to rot,
The tallest, roundest, fullest plant
By far to grace my garden plot,
Born to dazzle and enchant—

The tallest, roundest, fullest plant
Of the four that started life that day,
All born to dazzle and enchant
By the vibrant light of early May.

Of the four that started life that day,
She was the one predestined to grow
By leaps in the blustery gusts of May—
Not Tanya or Nancy or Jackie O.

Barbara was preordained to grow
In the rich, dark, made-to-order soil,
Though Tanya, Nancy and Jackie O
Also dined on salmon oil.

In the rich, dark, made-to-order soil,
With ample water and sunshine galore,
They thrived on Alaskan salmon oil,
Happy as kids in a candy store.

With ample water and sunshine galore,
They sprouted buds and bent from the weight,
Plump as kids in a candy store—
Until they were slapped by the hand of fate.

The buds, their branches bent with weight,
Were whipped about in a furious gale.
Jackie's limbs were stripped—by fate,
Tanya and Nancy proved equally frail.

Whipped about in the howling gale,
Barbara escaped with one measly snag.
While Harding and Kerrigan proved frail,
They and Jackie produced all the swag.

Our star escaped with one small snag—
But hold on, that's another story.
Before her buds began to flag,
Barbara Bush was bound for glory.

Willie's Wine

I know when I store wine in Willie's cellar,
As it gains age it blooms as Willie's wine.
My ripe Château d'Yquem is his "Old Yeller,"
My Château Lafite-Rothschild simply "Mine."
So why do I persist in asking Willie
To let me keep my precious bottles there?
Premier grand cru or muscadelle from Chile,
I am the only one with whom he'll share.
Like Carpenter and Walrus in a coma,
We swallow oysters by the boiling sea,
Discussing Châteauneuf-du-Pape's aroma
And wallowing in my mature Chablis.
His wine or mine, we circumvent a crisis
By popping corks and toasting Dionysus.

Gravity & Greed

Rich People

Rich people haven't got a clue to life.
They either have or are a trophy wife.
Their progeny can't scratch a simple itch
Without proclaiming "Look at me, I'm rich!"
They almost always dress before they dine
And have a sommelier to serve their wine,
A chef to orchestrate their haut cuisine,
A chauffeur for their custom limousine,
An upstairs maid to rectify their mess
And help the lady of the house undress,
A kitchen maid who's fair of shape and face
And doesn't mind succumbing to the chase.
They sit on boards and give to charities
Oblivious to life's disparities.

The Trickle-up Theory

No matter how you divvy up the pie,
Demand is bound to overtake supply.
There's only so much dough to go around.
This drives us job creators to the ground.

The ninety-nine percent are trying to steal
A bigger slice, and we've begun to feel
The pinch. We're forced to keep our year-old yachts
When next year's models promise sixty knots.

We need our villas in the south of France,
Our island hideaways where we can dance
And play, our Swiss chalets, our Central Park
Apartments, mansions like East Hampton's Arc.

To those who say there's something wrong with greed,
We say, *To each according to his need!*
Our need to feed our offshore bank accounts
In exponential leaps to keep amounts

Ahead of spending has us on the edge.
Instead of jumping off a Wall Street ledge,
We choose to squeeze the poor, the sick, the old,
And turn their abject suffering to gold

With subsidies and tax breaks from our friends
In Congress and the Highest Court, whose ends
Do justify the means, however sordid and perverse
They seem to those who shake their fists and curse.

We billionaires have placed a hammerlock
On all the wealth, but malcontents who squawk
Will praise us to the heavens when we spread
Good will by making sure old folks are fed,

Poor folks have heat in winter, and the ill
Have relatives prepared to foot the bill.
The unemployed will laud us when they learn
The sky's the limit to how much they'd earn

If only they'd been born with ample means
And other measures of their family's genes.
Democracy's passé. Without debate,
We privateers have seized the Ship of State.

How to Feed the Hungry

My plan's to round up billionaires
And lock them tight in feedlot pens
Until they're fat as Frigidaires,
Then do them in like Tyson hens.

Once these elites play out, my plan's
To tackle multimillionaires
And package them in quart-sized cans
To make sure everybody shares.

Their children, born to lives of ease,
Will spare themselves their parents' fate
By paring down necessities
And loving what they thought they'd hate:

A Murphy bed with squeaky springs
Above a Brooklyn butcher shop
And eating out at Burger Kings
And drinking diet soda pop.

The Fifteen Commandments

with a nod to Mel Brooks

When God gave Moses the three tablets, He thought He'd covered all the bases. The third tablet, the one Moses broke on his way down from Mount Sinai, foresaw the necessity to keep future kings from destroying the birds in the air and the fish in the sea, not to mention the clean air and water.

He had labored over life on Earth for endless days. He was afraid some brainless idiot would destroy His handiwork in the blink of an eye, biblically speaking, not that the progeny of Adam and Eve had paid that much attention to the Ten Commandments that survived the trip down the mountain, *Thou shalt not commit adultery* being one prime example.

Moses broke the two remaining tablets when he saw how the children of Israel danced like idolaters, bowing before the golden calf, giving God the finger. Who could blame him? With nothing to show for forty days and forty nights, plus six he spent in the dark cloud, he got Joshua to help reconstruct the tablets from scratch, pacing and muttering while Joshua waited with chisel ready and hammer poised.

"Thou shalt not covet ... what? I know it like the back of my hand, covet, covet ... thy neighbor's house, I knew it was in there somewhere. And, thou shalt not covet thy neighbor's wife, which seems redundant, given the whole adultery bit. Or his male or female servant, his ox or his ass, make that donkey, or anything that is thy neighbor's. Period. Oy vey!"

Ashamed to admit he'd broken the third tablet, he called it a day. But his dreams were plagued by locusts and enormous whirlwinds, wildfires, periods where fields withered to dust, floods you were lucky to escape with the shirt on your back.

Bouncing Bareback Baby Boomers

Headline: *Gas prices drive man to commute by horse.*

Headline: *Bakery makes deliveries with horse-drawn wagon to beat gas prices.*

Now comes news that market forces—
Laissez-faire-type economics—
Soon will find us riding horses
As we lose our crude oil sources,
Fueling jokes by late-night comics

Percherons will soon be spotted
Hitched to SUVs and pickups
Parked outside the Food Mart. Potted
Palms will sprout where gas pumps squatted.
Guards will loom, alert for stickups.

Picture rush hour: Horse commuters
By the thousands standing idle
When some hip-hop dudes on scooters
Bound for Happy Hour at Hooters
Tangle with a gelding's bridle.

Highway travel will to some seem
Wondrous, weird and wildly witty.
Visualize a 20-mule team
Caravan of shiny Airstream
Trailers tooling through Sioux City.

Bouncing bareback baby boomers
Proud astride their painted ponies—
All-time consummate consumers
Sporting Neiman-Marcus bloomers—
Will host Wild West shows for cronies.

Horse Marines will bite the dusty
Trail as caissons go on rolling.
Mothballed Humvees will turn rusty—
Same for tanks and other trusty
Weapons. Wars will stop for foaling.

The Battle of Mount Narcissus

Two gods upon a summit, standing toe-
To-toe, hurl insults at the other's bod:
"You have such tiny little hands, you so-
And-so!" says one. "And you are deeply flawed,"
The other says, "a bloated hot-air blimp!"
"Your mother mated with a head of cheese!"
Says one. "Your father was a cocktail shrimp,"
The other says, "and ravaged by disease!"
On Mount Narcissus, all gods look and talk
Alike, and shake their swords and shields of brass.
Sparks fly when arch-combatants strut and mock
The prancing peacock in the looking glass.
"You have the aura of a garbage dump!"
Says one. The other snorts and bellows, "Schlump!"

In Praise of Billionaires

You've got to hand it to the billionaires
Or they will send their minions round to take it.
They write the rules: Whatever's yours is theirs,

What's theirs is stashed in offshore banks to make it
Vanish when the taxman comes to call.
The burden falls on you who cannot fake it

With loopholes, credits, and deferrals, all
Designed to guarantee that no one shares
The wealth who's not already made a haul.

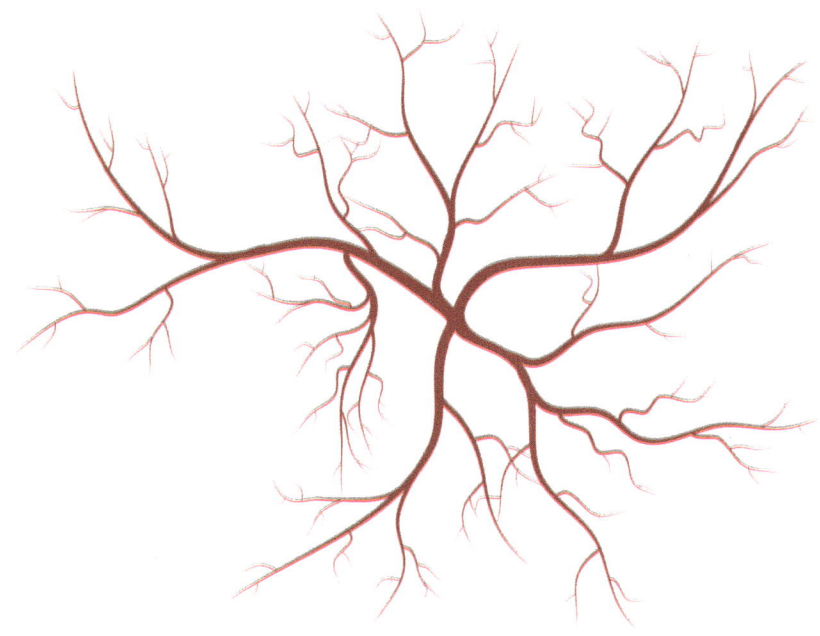

Literature & Lore

The Poetaster

The diehard poetaster shows distaste
For formal meters not precisely paced.
His measured lines are by inversions graced,
His words, for EMPHASIS, are uppercased,
His past and present tenses interlaced,
His semicolons frequently; misplaced,
His fulgent adjectives assumed in haste,
His hackneyed images best off effaced.
Oblivious to critics who lambaste
His sentiments as saccharine or chaste,
His feeble stabs at metaphor a waste,
He dotes upon the mistress he's embraced.
He doesn't mind when critics say his verse
Belongs on greeting cards; he could do worse.

A Guide to the Modern Sonnet

Erase old-fashioned notions from your mind,
Frivolities like rhyme, unless it's slant,
And meter, because meter is a grind—
A kiss of death when going for a grant.
Now let your nimble fingers wade at will
In pools of unadulterated thought.
Express your inmost contradictions, spill
Your beans—but stick to business: Thou shalt not,
On penalty of death, write fourteen lines.
It's over, baby. Modern won the war.
Gone are the brick walls with the ivy vines.
New waves knock against the rocky shore.
Couplets, once considered groups of two,
Now stretch from none at all to quite a few.

Ballade for the Birthday of Cyrano at the Coffee Time Coffee Shop

with apologies to Edmond Rostand

No words do justice to this grand affair
Beyond what Cyrano declared: How *fate,*
The arbitrator, *loves a jest!* Voltaire
Would blush to see how people celebrate
The birthday of a man who made his date
With Death wait while he gave his flame a ring,
A rosy dot over the i of Loving,
His nose aglow, red as Pinocchio's
When tendering his lies *like thin smoke rising.*
Ah! Whose nose plucks your heartstrings? Cyrano's!

Unless you're rocking in a straight-back chair,
You scratch your head attempting to relate
To Cyrano's restraint. Who's not aware
These days that plastic surgery's cut-rate?
No need for noses to *protuberate*
Like perches for the birds that come to sing,
Or *blue cucumbers,* say, or anything
Like *razor-cases* or *portfolios.*
Just whack 'em back to where they're ravishing.
Ah! Whose nose plucks your heartstrings? Cyrano's!

What is this thing called Love but nature's snare?
He queries, tête-à-tête with musket mate
Le Bret. Let every flitting bug beware:
Though dazzling light displays may fascinate,
The heat of contact will incinerate
The foxy one as well as the unwitting.
Yet Roxane fritters Love away while kissing
De Bergerac's frayed billets-doux, her woes
Compounded by the dividend she's missing.
Ah! Whose nose plucks your heartstrings? Cyrano's!

Those pretty nothings that are everything,
Those winds of jealous beauty ever blowing
Their dark fire and their music—God help those
Who pass Love by with Truth and Beauty glowing.
Ah! Whose nose plucks your heartstrings? Cyrano's!

In Praise of Peter Sellers

If Jacques Clouseau had soared across the moat
Like James Bond, harnessed in a parasail,
No need for pole vault, hook-and-rope, or boat,
He would have "lockéd Dreyfus in the gaol"
In less time than it takes to "stir, not shake"
The perfect dry martini. Laughing gas,
The plastic nose, the havoc in his wake,
The madcap bugle call at Khyber Pass . . .
No Chance of *Being There?* No Doctor Strange-
Love beating back his lust? No Doctor Pratt?
No RAF Group Captain Mandrake? Change
The Mouse That Roared and *What's New, Pussycat?*
Sean Connery's a draw, but count the cost,
The hours of belly-busting laughter lost.

The Crosscut in the Crotch

When loggers take a whiskey break
They scratch their underwear,
And without fail one starts a tale
So real you feel you're there.

The tree was young when Cutter hung
His crosscut in the crotch.
MacDonald said, *That pecker's dead,*
And swigged a slug of Scotch.

Then Murphy yelled, *Some quick lick felled*
A blue dick outlaw tree!
All hands and the cook and the whiskey jacks!
A bull of the woods was he.

They all took off like whooping cough.
The gill-poked kid was fine.
The crosscut stayed where it was laid
Astride an Oregon pine.

That highball team spilled jersey cream
Like water from a well.
When they moved on, the old growth gone,
They put a patch on hell.

Nobody knew the tree still grew.
It kept on adding rings
Until the saw was swallowed raw,
Its handles spread like wings.

One day some greenhorn chanced to lean
His chainsaw steel-to-steel,
And in his hearse was heard to curse
From Moosejaw to Mobile.

Expressions drawn from *Woods Words: A Comprehensive Dictionary of Loggers Terms,* by Dean Walter F. McCulloch, School of Forestry, Oregon State College, published by the Oregon Historical Society and The Champoeg Press, 1958, introduction by Stewart Holbrook.

The Moon on the Moss Beneath the Virgin

"It was like saying goodbye to a ***statue.***"
—*Ernest Hemingway*

Their time together had ended too ***soon,***
As with all first meetings between ***those***
Who would be lovers, and when their ***passion***
Rose in the second summer of their ***love,***
In a bed of moss between gray granite ***slabs***

In the small cimitero outside ***Finale,***
They laughed, not at love, or the ***sun***
Burning a bright hole through the ***overcast,***
But at the painted eyes, robin's egg ***blue,***
Staring down at them from the ***birdspecked***

Image of the Virgin. "Why does she ***watch***
With a small smile?" Pia asked, ***drawing***
A finger, its nail a nub, through the ***damp***
Crease beneath her left breast. "Do ***you***
Not know?" Amo said, propping his ***head***

On an elbow and gazing hard at the ***soft***
Features of the Virgin. The sun ***glared***
Down without mercy as she stared ***beyond***
The white sky, puzzling. "No," she ***said.***
He grinned. "There was a time when ***you***

Would have known, columba mia, a ***time***
Before us when you would have ***known.***"
"But was there time before us, or was ***there***
Just the sun?" She remembered the ***lazy***
Sun that first summer when they would ***meet***

At Harry's Bar, and he would order **Livorno**
Al forno, laughing through tears. **Pollo**
Al forno, she would tell the **waiter,**
Each time lifting the black veil she **wore**
As a symbol of mourning for her **beloved**

Ami, and clucking her tongue. And the **hazy**
Sun that autumn afternoon when they **kissed**
Farewell to summer in each other's **arms.**
"A crazy old sun," he said, drawing ***fingers,***
One after another, through the damp **crease**

Beneath her right breast. "A sun for **all**
Seasons." "A fun sun," she teased. "A **hon**
Of a sun." He grabbed her and rolled **her**
Over in the moss, over and over, until **she**
Cried and laughed, and begged him to **stop.**

And they lay still for a time, and **soon**
The moon rose behind the Virgin and the **small**
Smile faded. "There was also the **moon,"**
He said softly. "Si, that is so," she **sighed,**
"But over my Ami, the moon rises no **more."**

The Dillowy Danderhonk

The Danderhonk in the Deacon's well
One day began to swell ... and swell.
With no direction to go but up,
It rose and rose till the Deacon's cup
Ran over and all the townsfolk came
To wonder who in blank was to blame
For the dillowy Danderhonk.

In a blink it swallowed the Deacon's wife,
Who came at it waving a gravy knife,
Then the Deacon's dog and all he owned.
When it got his cat the Deacon groaned,
For gone was his little pride and joy,
The love of his life, his baby boy,
To the depths of the Danderhonk.

The beast spilled into a neighbor's yard
And turned the poor man's pigs to lard.
The townsfolk wrung their hands and prayed
As the Danderhonk advanced and made
A mockery of the dinkers they tossed,
Whose purpose, if one existed, was lost
In the flanks of the Danderhonk.

When the creature reached the edge of town,
The Grand Wyzee donned cap and gown
To pace up and down discussing the case
Of the Danderhonk's abuse of space.
Meanwhile the Deacon drowned his woes
At the Rub-a-Dub Pub to protect his nose
From the stink of the Danderhonk.

The townsfolk threw up their hands and fled
When the beast, by slow degrees, turned red
As the dimpled face of a cranberry bog
And spread like fleas on the Deacon's dog.
There was nothing anyone knew how to do
To stop the monster, and so it grew
To the dandiest Danderhonk.

Then a wisp of a miss came up and kissed
The Danderhonk and made it list,
And swoon, and shrink, and faint dead away,
And turn from a rosy hue to gray.
The beast, it appeared, had fed on fear,
And the girl, to be fair, shed a tiny tear
For the ghost of the Danderhonk.

In Pursuit of My Beautiful Muse

I run dribbling off with my fountain pen
Spitting profundities—*rat-tat-tat-tat-tat!*—
Repeating redundancies over and over again,
Spotting the hollow, speckling the glen,
Until, like Bartholomew Cubbins's last hat,

A word appears as if by magic in my path:
A trillium aglow on moss in a misted wood . . .
Venus stepping unattended from her bath . . .
The dawn's eye opening over the aftermath
Of snow . . . apple pie, the flag, motherhood . . . .

I shake the pen. The word withers to thin
Air—*poof!*—like that. Evaporates. Is gone.
Cursing with the rough tongue Rumpelstiltskin
Laid on the golden maid with an awful grin
In the grip of his greed, I run dribbling on.

Halfway back to the blasted gate—*blink!*—
Tinkerbell dances forth in tights and tutu,
Skates figure-eights, prances about the rink,
And with a view to what lies ahead (to think!)
Writes my missing word in the glittering dew.

Again I shake the pen. My star-studded word
Flutters like hearts when a slumbering Earth
Stretches and yawns—*zoom!*—like a hummingbird
Humming the bumblebee flight song, an absurd
Little wind-up butterfly. I sense rebirth.

The word quivers like neon Jell-O on a spoon,
Strawberry, Grape, every flavor in the book,
Cherry to Lemon-Lime, Passion Fruit to Prune.
A trio of bobolinks whistles *Clair de Lune.*
Nag and ninny rush the rail for a closer look

As skyrockets shock and electrify the zodiac
With spectacular flashes of pyrotechnic skill.
My pen flares, and from it flows crackerjack
Prose. Praising the bright, unbridled maniac
In the Moon's face, tumbling after like Jill

(For the thrill!), I steeplechase my Muse
Through dazzling depth and over heady crest,
Throwing off shirt, pants, socks and shoes,
Warbling chanteys, tapping hornpipe tattoos
On a shoulder of Earth, a buttock, a breast,

Laughing like Looney Tunes, my lines undone
The way the strings of Brahms spill sound,
The water lilies of Monet collect the sun,
The pen of Tennyson outpaces Wellington.
I race a fast track!—I am triple-crowned!

Kick the Can

for Adelaide Crapsey

Bash it.
Kick the damn can
To Kansas. Beat it all
To hell. Take a sledgehammer and
Smash it.

Love & Lust

Stagestruck

When I think of time lost
My life in arrears
Whole hours days weeks
Months entire years
Where I let love be
Swallowed in the rush
The soft served fast
Like breakfast mush
Careening as I was
Off my life's careers
Carrying weights
Of no measure like fears
Laid on fears till they're
One in the crush
And I wish on wish
Wanting only to brush
Someone feminine's cheek
Taste lover's tears
You step on stage
To my whistles and cheers

Relativity

There's no way to measure
The relative pleasure
Of two hearts aflutter.

What's good for the boy'll
Be good for the goil,
A hot knife through butter.

They'll tickle their parents
With talk of foreswearance
Until they st-stutter.

No matter how careful
They are, they'll be prayerful
Whenever they putter.

Three Limericks with Titles

The Ban Rolls On

A young Zoroastrian friend
Prays Ahura Mazda will send
A girl who will close
Her eyes and her nose
For bathing's tabooed by the Zend.

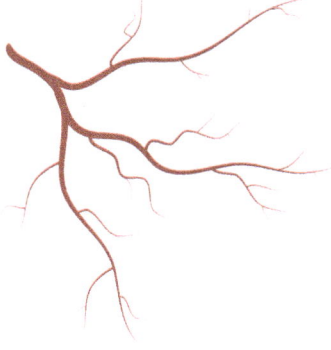

Pound Foolish

When young Dr. Carpenter failed
To heed an old saw he got nailed.
"Penny wise!" the nurse cried
As he hammered and pried.
Her dad, Dr. Byrd, had him jailed.

Bottom Line

He eyeballed the minivan's sticker.
His wife and the salesman grew thicker.
He said, "Sure be nice
If you whittled the price
But I won't try to force you to dicker."

Only Mnemosyne Knows

Did the gods of Greek mythology
Copulate like mere mortals, or did they
Levitate in the rarefied air above Mount Olympus
Like ruby-throated hummingbirds at a patio feeder,
Waving their feathered fans to stay aloft?

Did they invoke some ephemeral form
Of kenosis, relinquishing their immortality
To taste the little death we humans know after
Sneezing or making love? Did they sow secrets
In the clouds for those splayed naked in the grass?

Did they will their proclivity for lust
To souls who lie supine beneath curly hairs
Of cirrus, cumulonimbus mammatus dangling ranks
Of Z-cupped curves, pileus slipping smooth-skinned
Skullcaps over rollicking thunderheads?

Did Zeus and Mnemosyne come together
Once for every Muse, or once in one basket,
Her eggs the envy of hen house and fertility clinic?
Did they do it standing, or astride a balance beam,
Or tumbling arse over tit in the fluffy clouds?

God Bless the Virgins

"He did not want the apple
for the apple's sake."
—*Mark Twain*

God bless the virgins
    for only virgins hold out
        hope. Salvation comes
            in many forms for them.

        God bless the virgins
      for too great a taste
    brings pain to the head
and sighs to the lips.

God bless the virgins
    for innocence gives rise
        to a man's respect. Balls
            are held to honor them.

The Curious Stares and the Hungry Eyes

My lips aquiver in the aftermath
Of love upon a brisk December eve
Beneath a drafty afghan—first the bath
And then the icy cold of cotton sleeve
And sock—I sing falsetto, laugh and dance,
And grip my parts against the sudden freeze,
The sheer euphoric shock, as underpants
Precipitate a plunge of some degrees—
And then I see them, fixed as in a trance,
Their eyes like windows open to my deeds,
These little witnesses to my romance
With one they worship to appease their needs.
We took a chance and promised to be fast,
But dinnertime arrived and rolled on past.

I'd Rather Sail My Schooner than Have Sex

We trace our roots to 1969
When Woodstock broke the mold. Make love not war.
Take one small step for man. Drink mellow wine.
Move boats to Idaho before the shore-
Line shifts and Boise fills your telescope.
Think meadows where vast herds of hippies graze
Contented with the grass like antelope.
How sweet the green, how brown the heavy haze.
We skip the slippery underwater rocks
Full speed upon a landlocked odyssey
Where risks enough to knock our Birkenstocks
Off filter through the fishnet filigree.
I'd rather sail my schooner than have sex
Except when you sign on to swab the decks.

Aubade: Dialogue at Dawn

Stay in this light, but let me see you faced
Away, a burnished copper goblet pressed
Against the gauzy sky, the pale blue laced
With apricot. And though I seem obsessed
With shape, I mean to underscore my haste
To understand the grandeur of your breast,
Whose glories go on glowing in the taste
Of what my lips, like fingertips, caressed
With syllables, my hands about your waist,
Describing you, deliciously undressed.

*My terra cotta friend, you dive as deep
As mind can fathom. How am I to choose
Between the boredom of a dreamless sleep
And a chance to dance holes in my shoes?
Now we must take our places with the sheep,
The puzzled ones who fail to spot the clues.
Let's lay our heads upon our hearts, and weep
The fates, and curse the tides, and sing the blues,
And rave, and crowd in line at Lover's Leap.
Or better, set another date, and make adieux.*

I like the sound of "terra cotta friend,"
Evocative of Earth. True friends are those
Who stand like rocks behind you to the end,
Who cling like mussels in the ebbs and flows
Of incident and circumstance, who bend
Like sea anemones. A lover grows
By magic, sprouting like a dividend,
A split, a crocus poking through the snows.
I shun the stock clichés of cattle penned
in lots, their empty eyes and bovine lows.

You are the driver off of all my fears,
The fan who never tires or loses zeal,
The floor stick I grab hold of, shifting gears,
The squirrel knob I use to spin the wheel
When cornering, to see how sweet it steers,
The leather seat I test for fit and feel,
A classic waxed with passion over years,
A cherry on the used car lot, a steal.
You grace my hood, an ornament with ears.
My nighttime road conditions bide ideal.

We lilt like Benedict and Beatrice
In Berlioz's singing valentine,
Rekindling Shakespeare's myth of married bliss
With varied tweaks and twists: The monkeyshine,
The pressure to approach the precipice,
Devotion to a fault, a taste for wine.
Before our winged epistles fly amiss,
Let's pop champagne and warble Auld Lang Syne.
Farewell for now, with this, my parting kiss.
Tomorrow night, same time, same place, online.

Bronze Bosom Above Mahogany Inboard Runabout

Colleen's good fortune was her family's wealth,
Enabler of her vintage runabout,
Her cocoa-butter tan, her teeth, her health,
The extra pounds she packed from dining out.
No criticism of the extra pounds
That gravitated to her splendid chest
And made her bosom spill beyond its bounds,
Inviting fantasies of her undressed.
I was the startled one when she swapped ends
And throttled down, making her runabout bob,
Her heavenly bosom bathed (the thought transends)
In shimmering light. "New nose?" I said. "Nice job."
I don't aspire to dabble in her league.
My light is beeswax candle, hers is klieg.

Puppy Love

Owners know the drill. The list
Begins with Number Fifty-five,
Which deals with getting roundly kissed
When all you want to do is drive.

From Number Twenty-seven on,
Complaints have more to do with holes
Dug randomly across the lawn
Between the earthen mounds of moles,

Barf on the pristine passenger seat
Of your brand-new car on the way to the vet,
Whose ministrations, incomplete,
Push you deeper into debt,

Teeth like needles through your shoe,
Muddy paw prints done for fun.
Number One is Number Two.
Number Two is Number One.

A Sunday Drive

She read my rosy prose and said *Surprise!*
To my surprise. I posed a writer's pose,
A mind to marvel sight through writers' eyes,
To tap a dance, to dance on writers' toes.

I wrote, and spoke as if I'd never write
Again. Again she buttoned up her coat,
Alluded to the dying of the light
And bade me rise, a muffler to my throat.

We drove familiar roads, a Sunday drive
Past river, greenway trail and alder grove,
The earth aglow, the vibrant leaves alive
With light, the sky a pirate's treasure trove.

We slowed to watch the fat sun dip and slide
In slivers down the sharp horizon, mowed
Like rows of amber grass, and she, wide-eyed
With wonder, cried *Ride on!* and on we rode.

Oh You!

You are my *joie de vivre*, dear,
The sunrise to my chanticleer—
For you inspire full-blown desire
As if it were your life's career!

You are my tenor saxophone,
My clarinet, my slide trombone—
The Dixieland of my jazz band,
My *Downbeat* and my *Rolling Stone!*

You are my cakes and ale, true-blue,
My cup of tea, my saucer, too—
In sum, the dish of my last wish,
My ripe Chablis, my oyster stew!

I'm with You

You don't know where
you're going, where you've
been. Neither do I,
I'm with you.

I'm an existentialist,
I've always been.
That's why I love now,
I'm with you.

Health & Happiness

Little Incubator

Every time my grandson comes to stay
He carries more than lessons in his head,
And leaves a keepsake when he goes away.

His school's ground zero for the vast array
Of rhinoviruses I've learned to dread
Every time my grandson comes to stay.

At recess when he scampers out to play
Mutations of the common cold are bred—
My latest keepsakes. When he goes away

He rides to school and back in pods that weigh
Ten tons, the means by which the bugs are spread.
Every time my grandson comes to stay

I greet him with a bear hug. I could say
Kiss off to winter visits, but instead
Accept the keepsakes when he goes away.

I keep my cabinet stocked with nasal spray
And plan to spend at least three days in bed
Every time my grandson comes to stay
And leaves a keepsake when he goes away.

'Tis the Season

A bird has all the breaks, I'm told,
For when his nose is nipped by cold
And frost appears, and leaves are blown,
It's never "He has flu"—he's flown.

Limerick

If you've heard that bird flu is serious
Here's word that'll drive you delirious
    A strain's been created
    That spreads unabated
The ways of mankind are mysterious

Vector Control

News item: *A novel scheme to repel mosquitoes and combat the diseases they spread with lasers is being funded by the world's second-richest man.*

Now we learn from scientific sources
About a threat to humans, cows, and horses.
Mosquitoes have their hands—feet, if you please—
On new technologies to spread disease.

The government is mum on how the bugs
Acquired their weapons. Were they running drugs,
Perhaps, or did a foreign power conspire
To tip their snouts with focused beams of fire?

Good thing the planet's second-richest man
Is pouring money into someone's plan
To stop the menace threatening our shores
Before we're banished from the out-of-doors.

A man that rich would profit from the yield
Of some invention, say a Vector Shield,
A skin protector, something state of the art—
Or tax wise, should the venture fall apart.

Willow Creek Hot Springs

I contemplate the tanned-all-over man,
Fly swatter poised to do what swatters do,
Who sits outside his faded white Ford van

Like some exalted potentate. His fan
Attacks a random insect, runs it through.
I contemplate the tanned-all-over man,

Aware how disbelief and umbrage can
Deflate an expectation. Here he knew
He'd sit outside his faded white Ford van

Spread-eagled, working on his world-class tan
With no intruders save a snake or two.
I contemplate the tanned-all-over man

Whose eyes pop egg-like from his frying pan
When grumbles come—his wife is in a stew.
She sits inside their faded white Ford van

Where temperatures approach Afghanistan,
legs crossed against a prying eye. In lieu,
I contemplate the tanned-all-over man

And ponder what had seemed a perfect plan—
Mid-August, miles from nowhere. Eyes askew,
He contemplates the tanned-all-over man
Who stands outside his faded white Ford van.

Georgine's Abrupt Recovery

With morphine the press of a button away,
Georgine was enjoying her hospital stay.
Her nurse, smiling down, said "We laid odds you'd croak.
Two weeks in a coma before you awoke!"

Georgine burst out laughing, then grimaced as pain
Shot forth from her suture and surged toward her drain.
A press of the button soon brought her around.
The drug was like liquor, though quicker, she found.

One morning, her nurse brought a washcloth and said,
"Here, freshen your face before breakfast in bed."
But breakfast meant only one thing to Georgine:
A press of the button—a shot of morphine.

Hurling the washcloth, a major league pitch,
The nurse smacked Georgine in the face and yelled *"Bitch!"*
The sting of the washcloth!—the insult unfurled!
Georgine sat up, wide-eyed, and rejoined the world.

Unreality Show

I went to see my dotty wife
Who's off her noggin and dreamy.
She didn't know me from Mack the Knife
But was happy as hell to see me.

She couldn't wait for me to meet
The love of her life, O'Reilly,
Who's half her height but twice as sweet
And fourteen times as smiley.

Waking Up in Willoughby

Think of movie stars from other eras
Stripping to their underwear and kissing
In your kitchen. Pick a perfect pair, as
Bogart and Bacall were. Think of wishing
On a star, and singing in the rain, and
Waking up in Willoughby where you get
Off, believing here at last's the mainland
After pitch and yaw, and surly crew. Let
Mind's eye wander tinseled streets in back lots,
Conjure ways to tease the spellbound lovers
Strewn about your schooner, stiff the crackpots,
Snatch the gold rings, lounge beneath the covers,
Drift like bobbers on a pond, loft streamers
Rippling on a draft, ally with dreamers.

A Fleeting Thought

There was no joy like mine, I had a thought

The thought got up and sauntered out the door

A thought will slither in and slip its arms

I'm left to splash about in afterglow

Around me, melting my resistance with its charms,

Of wisdom so profound, so weighty, so

Leaving me sobbing on the kitchen floor.

Like none before it in my time, one fraught

With nuances—but now I am distraught.

It's happened so damned many times before—

Then disappear before it trips alarms.

Nouveau—and now no one will ever know.

Life is a Beach

"I'm going to stay with you
And we won't worry what to do"
—T.S. Eliot

Life is a beach, and we but grains
Of sand over which little sand fleas hop.
The season waxes, then it wanes;
As we promenade from shop to shop,

Pressing our noses to windowpanes,
We cast an ear as people pop
And crack with talk like scatterbrains,
Dulling the points of their lives with yawp.

When you and I throw off our chains,
We'll turn to stone and sit atop
A lofty peak, eying the plains
Adrift with mist, a serene backdrop

Free of the sea and its hurricanes,
Just the two of us, sharing an outcrop
With eagles and hawks, the filigreed veins
Of silver and gold our only sop

To vanity. And when the rains
Tear down our tower, drop by drop,
And glaciers stock their rock moraines,
We'll find another mountaintop.

Ah, the two of us!—despite our pains
We laugh and sing. Let fools flip-flop
And drown in down-and-out refrains,
Or strut as fanfaron or fop—

We shall endure. No fear profanes
The inner sanctum where we swap
Sweet fantasies. As love ordains,
All folly is a transient prop;

The tidepool fills and then it drains.
Though no one sees it start or stop,
The season waxes, then it wanes.
We cast an ear as people pop.

Nothing on Earth

A zipper's handy when a man
> Must sacrifice his self esteem
> And run like hell to find the can.

What in the ordinary scheme
> Of living seems so minor, so
> Pedestrian, becomes a theme:

When you gotta go, you gotta go,
> Quicker than you can bat an eye.
> Nothing on Earth is quite so slow—

Glancing left-right on the sly,
> Dancing about like Peter Pan—
> As fumbling with a button fly.

Business & Pleasure

Hog Tithe

If I had a dime
For every time
Some dumb schlemiel
Behind the wheel
Of an SUV
Cut in front of me
And then went slow
I'd be rolling in dough.

Dances with Marketeers

I pick up the phone and there's nobody there.
I know I'm about to be hustled
By somebody paid to shamefacedly care
If I had a nice day or tussled.

A click in my ear, then a phlegmatic voice
Recites what's been drummed in by trainers,
The icebreaker followed by one of a choice
Assortment of hackneyed no-brainers.

Insurance or time-share or luxury cruise,
I sharpen the quips in my quiver.
I start off by saying I'm drowning in booze,
And cirrhosis is eating my liver.

"The bankers who found me to be in arrears
Foreclose on my mortgage tomorrow.
You say there's no interest, no fees for five years?
No end to how much I can borrow?"

"Of course I would love to cut costs to the nub.
I jump at the chance to pinch pennies.
But would I fit in at an exercise club?
I can't afford gym shorts or tennies."

"Three days at a fat farm are just what I need.
Massages and saunas work wonders.
Keep bandages handy—my bedsores may bleed—
And diapers to cover my blunders."

"I can't wait to sail on your luxury cruise.
Six days in the sunny Bahamas!
The ladies will love my erotic tattoos—
I sleepwalk without my pajamas."

"Insurance to round out my meager estate?
It's something I've thought about buying.
Six million sounds perfect. Your timing is great!
My doctor just told me I'm dying."

*The ladies will love my erotic tattoos—
I sleepwalk without my pajamas.*

Facts Plucked from a Back-cover Ad

Every president from Hoover through
Bush Two has brought an entourage to stay
At the Arizona Biltmore. Guests can view
Them all in the hotel's noted History Hallway.

Marilyn Monroe lounged by the pool
Known as The Catalina for its tiles
From Catalina Island. As a rule,
Staff slipped past in random ranks and files.

The Biltmore and the Island both were bought
By chewing-gum magnate William Wrigley
Junior, master of the Turkey Trot,
Whose showgirls all were dimpled, blonde, and giggly.

Irving Berlin soaked up the Phoenix sun
While writing down "White Christmas." Stars
Like Sammy, Frank, and Liza, just for fun,
Staged concerts at the hotel's piano bars.

The Arizona Biltmore lobby boasts
A gold-leaf ceiling second only to
The Taj Mahal. No fresh reports of ghosts.
Almost every word of this is true.

The Chauffeur's Tale

"Far back in our dark soul the horse prances."
—*D.H. Lawrence*

I praise my lady's thighs
Her rhythmic breasts exposed
In amber streetlight strobe
When a writer friend arrives

And she alone drives in
To greet him at the train
And they dismiss the rain
And pass a flask of gin

And she lets drop her soul
As they plunge through the night
Immersed in the pulsing light
To a depth beyond control

While the plump assistant cook
Flutters about my plate
And the wisp of an upstairs maid
Featherdusts my hood.

Good Little Shoppers

We got along fine before Walmart
Made Main Street a thing of the past.
Then Amazon filled up our e-cart
And left even chain stores aghast.

The trend toward consumer eavesdropping
Reduces our choice of commodities.
We find as we go about shopping
A shortage of off-brands and oddities.

Thanks now to electronic spying
Retailers can compound their greed.
Too often we find ourselves buying
Whatever they tell us we need.

Life & Death

The Gospel of Fred

My crotchety compadre Fred
Was an atheist with a capital A.
"Give us this day our daily bread
But deliver us from God," he'd say.

"Remove religion from your life,
Let love become your hitching post."
This didn't sit well with his wife
Who entertained the Holy Ghost.

It fell to Grace to bury Fred
When he went belly up and froze
As people do when newly dead.
I praised the epitaph she chose:

HERE LIES FRED
ENTOMBED BUT FREE
OF HEAVEN ABOVE OR HELL BELOW
DOOMED TO SPEND ETERNITY
ALL DRESSED UP
WITH NOWHERE TO GO

HANGOVER

I dip my mug in recollection's all-
Too-deep repository of regret
And sip until my thoughts dissolve, then fall
Asleep and dream I've tumbled into debt.
My car is repossessed, my homestead's sold
To pay back taxes, and my wife's run off.
Bizarre, because I own my car, an old
Coupé with wide whitewalls, a chronic cough
And loads of chrome, a relic from the days
Of fins and fender skirts, and narrow two-
Lane roads where Plymouths, Fords and Chevrolets
Took spins. I bid my pride and joy adieu,
My life, my love, my little buttercup.
My wife is beaming down when I wake up.

Death Came to Me Last Night

Death came to me last night with bony hand
On high, walked through my door without a knock,
Stood like some cobweb-decorated clock
At Halloween. "It's Death!" I cried. "How grand
Of you to call!" I lied. "You're in demand!"
It's one thing to let Death blow past your lock,
Another to let Death deflate your stock.
"Send out for chicken strips! Strike up the band!"

It's not to say Death doesn't stake a claim
To all I leave behind, my *Rolling Stones,*
My beads, my meditations on the world,
But when Death came I camouflaged my name,
Struck up the clarinets and slide trombones,
Slipped out the back, and rode with flags unfurled.

When Audrey Sailed

The city lost a citizen whose forte
Was darting forth with dignity and dog
Bedecked, the skipper, hatted, hard aport,
The mate, in dainty little knitted tog,
Awash upon the window, starboard side.
The picture's one of her befurred with fox,
Powdered, rouged and veiled, a blushing bride,
The dog mustachioed, with curly locks.
I charted stars to cross her line of sight,
And every time we met, she made a pass;
I played Odysseus to her water sprite
In brief liaisons in the looking glass.
The city lost a citizen who sailed;
The dog and I, atop the lighthouse, wailed.

for Audrey Barry, 1910-1989

The Lonely Glove

She languishes alone in a dresser drawer
With reminiscences of how her mate
And she accented what their mistress wore
That wretched day when fickle-fingered fate,
With heavy hand, conspired to split the pair.
It was November, and the leaves had turned—
Vine maple, mountain ash, and scarlet oak
Ablaze with blush. A nip was in the air.
Their mistress, scribbling in her notebook, burned
The pages with her words, went home to soak.

Before submerging in her bath, she graced
Her vanity with gloves and woolen cap,
Slipped off the burden of her cloak and faced
Attentive mirrors, traced her contour map
From chin to ankle, gloried in her lines.
She (now the glove) watched helplessly as he,
Her mate, slid slowly from her anguished sight.
Fresh from her bath, their mistress, wines
And foods arrayed, went on a lyric spree.
But what of her (the glove's) unfolding plight?

This was no ordinary store-bought glove,
A dime a dozen on the bargain rack—
This was her finely tailored, hand-stitched love.
They lay together in a regal stack
On a countertop of brass and beveled glass
In an haut couture boutique in the south of France,
Where their mistress spent her summers writing verse.
Back home, she shared his warmth until—alas!—
Their mistress, caught up in Erato's trance,
Sent him to Goodwill in a cast-off purse.

A Good Day to Die

First check the weather report. A light drizzle is fine if you dress for it. Overcast is better, cloudy bright is best. Not too hot, you don't want to sweat. Next, pick a place with a pleasing aspect. Avoid venues where people congregate.

Someone invariably asks idiotic questions. Why did you choose this particular spot? Are you some kind of religious crank? Do you have insurance? This is the hard part.

People are everywhere. If you go to the beach, good luck finding an expanse of sand. Stand in the woods, ten to one you hear voices. Sit on the bank of a swift stream, huge rubber rafts thrust and plunge, heads perched atop life preservers scream, jet boats bellow like Roman bulls, fly fishers cast jaundiced eyes, hikers point zinc oxide noses.

Try some alcove close to home. Middle of the week, school in session. Bring along a small rug, the ground gets harder by the hour, rocks are impossible in a matter of minutes. Carry a water bottle. Nothing is worse than a dry mouth. Dry sinuses maybe.

And snacks. Fruit is great, especially berries in season, a baguette, your favorite cheese. And toilet paper just in case. Sit cross-legged if you're able, otherwise make yourself comfortable. Conjure scenes of your childhood, the more pleasurable times. Wish away your worst regrets.

Notice everything, mosses, amphibians, the inexorable creep of shadows, beauty beyond expression. Everyday stuff, there when you fold your rug and go home, there when you're gone forever.

Just Desserts

They planted a pig valve in Bob's heart.
He suffered sundry other ills.
His blood pressure rampaged off the chart.
He popped a panoply of pills.

Still, Marge was startled to stand and watch
Bob's eyes go blank and lose their lights.
She offered supper, a glass of Scotch
To the priest who read belated rites.

Stripping Bob down, she got undressed.
I'm free! From now on, no more men!
She danced a fandango on his chest.
I'll never be stuck with a man again!

Bob sat straight up and she dropped dead.
"Baby, you got that right," he said.

The Chair: Its Merits

Regarding the Chair, it
    behooves to compare it
with sometimes defective
    and thus incorrective
devices for dealing
    with murder and stealing.

The trouble with hanging,
    besides all the banging
while building a gibbet
    for public exhibit,
resides in the question
    of noisome egestion.

The danger in shooting
    is one of commuting
the sentence by aiming
    and carelessly maiming,
thus rousing a clamor
    to close down the slammer.

The bother of gassing
    begins with the passing
and ends when the waiting
    pays off, indicating,
to everyone's pleasure,
    an adequate measure.

The curse of injecting
    comes after selecting
a vein for the toxin
    and finding the doc's in
the deadlock of drippage
    and vascular slippage.

The Chair, you discover,
    is charged like a lover
who melts your resistance
    with heated persistence
and follows by mounting
    your final accounting.

Electrically courted,
    your circuits are shorted,
Your senses sent reeling
    as you begin feeling
Society's current
    orgasmic deterrent.

Age Appropriate

I wonder where I could be heading.
My kids are all grown up and gone.
My life is more funeral than wedding,
Less Vegas and more Forest Lawn.

War & Peace

Flight of the Iguana

Headline: *"Cat starts apartment fire; man's pet iguana is missing"*

The cat survived the one-alarmer
With only minor scrapes.
The blazing futon didn't harm her
The way it did the drapes.

According to the duo's owner,
Kitty was prone to play,
While Hugh, a feline-hating loner,
Wished the cat astray.

Kitty deemed Hugh an interloper
With spooky sea-green eyes,
A guttural-hissing slippery-sloper,
A creature to despise.

The cat, in the iguana's thinking,
Belonged in a holding tank
Exposed to steady strobe light blinking,
Spread-eagled on a plank.

Kitty construed Hugh's barroom brawling
As headed for a wreck.
Tipped like a dinghy in the squalling,
Hugh's heat lamp hit the deck.

Kitty, not ready for Nirvana,
Seizing her domain,
Catapulted Hugh Iguana
Beyond the astral plane.

The Pre-divorce Contract

It is, indeed, a dark and stormy night,
Though moonbeams daub the land, and dazzling stars
Reach deep inside their destinies for light.
At odds sit Eva Grimm and husband Lars,
Known to their closest friends as Muff and Stud,
She from her Venus traits, he from his Mars.

They face each other like two clumps of mud,
Laptops laid between the plates of lox,
Cream cheese and bagels, smart pens dripping blood.
Their made-in-heaven marriage on the rocks,
They do what clear-eyed couples do, to wit,
Divide the tax-free bonds and blue chip stocks

Themselves, list terms, provisos, recommit
Each other's soul to roam the Twilight Zone,
Assisted by a how-to-do-it kit.
At stake, of course, is everything they own.
He knows she craves his signed Pelé kneepads.
She's seen him sneak her Gucci mobile phone.

They stagger under commas, myriads
Of dashes; semi-colons spill from packs
Crammed full of ampersands and periods.
She reins in her propensity to wax
Baroque, effusive as a harpsichord.
He fiddles with his out-of-whack syntax.

Before a thought appears on-screen, a sword
Swoops down to slice plump sentences to bits;
Ripe words and letters tumble overboard.
He scowls and pouts as blind injustice splits
The balance sheet, while she starts throwing things,
Smashing small objects, having hissy fits.

Her shrink admonished her: "As spider clings
To fly, hang on for life." His clowned around:
"Best call a screeching halt to night-owl flings."

She wound up groping for esteem. He wound
Up suffocating. Vanished like a grain
Field thick with locusts was the middle ground

Where each might glean a soupçon, drop disdain
And strike a match, reflecting, in their strictures,
Opposing halves of their one scattered brain.
"It's all your father's fault," she gripes. "He lectures
Me like a servant." "It's your mother's, please,"
He snipes. "She paints outrageous verbal pictures."

He strokes the bronze they copped at Sotheby's,
A steal at twice the price. "I'll live with this."
She slaps his hand. "Like Mephistopheles!"
"Who recognized it as Rodin's 'The Kiss'?"
"But who said 'Here, Hot Lips, it's yours'? Who joked
How he hoped it jacked up whose wedded bliss?"

"Who pulled the bidding off?" he puffs. "Who poked
Who in the ribs?" she huffs. "Who grabbed whose hand
And raised it when who lost his pluck and choked?"
"Who had the *savoir-faire,*" he toots, "to stand?"
"Who goosed who after who," she hoots, "had floated
Like Tinkerbell off into Neverland?"

"Who signed the check?" he chortles. "But who toted
Two tons of metal to the van," she snorts,
"While who leaped to the counter top and gloated?"
The hours whiz past with chockablock retorts
Flung toe-to-toe, a knock-down-drag-out bout
Worthy of Philistines crocked in their forts.

Slings snap and bowstrings twang, cartouches sprout
About the Persian rug like blasphemies,
The bloody outcome all the while in doubt.
There is one clause on which the pair agrees:
Drafting the contract hand-in-hand, they write
Off lawyers, bypass courts, and keep the fees.

The Spartans Versus the Athenians

The football game was scheduled by mistake.
Big Ten teams don't smack pads with lesser schools.
Athena College reveled at the break

By seizing opportunities to make
A statement obvious to fops and fools:
The football game was scheduled by mistake.

The Spartan coaches chortled *Piece of cake!*
Their guards and tackles packed the kicks of mules.
Athena College reveled at the break

When trustees met, and for decorum's sake,
Dropped *ball* and *body contact* from the rules.
The football game was scheduled by mistake

But Spartan celebration turned to wake—
Their guards and tackles lacked the verbal tools.
Athena College reveled at the break;

Since intellect's impossible to fake,
Their scoreboard points piled up like molecules.
The football game was scheduled by mistake!
Athena College reveled at the break.

Politics & Bureaucracy

Airport Insecurity

A pox upon airport security planners
Whose paucity of common sense and manners
Subjects our flabby flesh to bawdy scanners.

We who opt to fly the friendly skies
Must stand stark naked in their prying eyes
Or drop our underdrawers and spread our thighs.

Invading privacy's a sticky wicket—
The ACLU thinks it isn't cricket—
But checkers view the scans as just the ticket:

They think we passengers should entertain
Them since their daily grind is so mundane.
"Besides, you folks can always take the train."

The TSA's gone nuts. Next thing you know,
They'll host a Fox TV reality show
Entitled "Bare-Ass Naked Head to Toe."

The TV screen will split between the strippers
And the gropers grappling with the zippers.
No one's spared—old geezers, little nippers.

We can, of course, abolish this tomfool-
Ery: Strap Congress in a ducking stool—
Make 'em agree to live by the Golden Rule.

We'll snicker at how quickly Congress tackles
An issue guaranteed to raise their hackles:
Their stuff subjected to guffaws and cackles.

Curbside Complaint

The city has a new composting plan
That renders obsolete the garbage can.
Putrescibles, known on the farm as "slops,"
Add color to the Mayor's photo ops.

Holding aloft a curbside pail, he touts
The benefits to people plagued with doubts—
Two-thirds, according to the latest poll
Of local citizens, who, on the whole,

Are shocked and awed as funding meant for schools
And filling potholes disappears. "What fools
These politicians be," the pollster quoted
From his notes. "Bureaucracy is bloated

To exploding," he continued. "Waste-
Ful spending's rampant, blah-blah-blah. We're faced
With higher taxes, yaddah-yah—" "You will
Get used to separating out your swill,"

The Mayor swore. "This bucket's neat and clean.
Environmentally, the city's green."
His microphone was hot when someone said,
"So what, if fiscally the city's red?"

"Fort Wayne Scratches Harry Baals"
—New York Daily News

Citizens picked the name in a poll.
Harry Baals beat Thunder Dome.
Fort Wayne's electorate's humor's droll,
Sophisticated, yet downhome.

But a building named for Harry Baals?
Said Mayor Henry: "Not on my watch!
Think of the spate of anonymous calls,
The jokes about the city's crotch."

Citizens had a right to groan
When Mayor Henry tipped the scales.
Baals was the best mayor Fort Wayne's known.
(Descendants claim the name is "Bales.")

"Harry Baals" would have been the seat
 Of government, but "Citizens Square"
 Was picked. Revenge was swift and sweet—
 It's known on the street as "The Square with Hair."

The Texas School Board Tackles Geography

The Earth is flat.

And that is that.

About the Author

David Hedges (shown with his ventriloquist's dummy, Deadpan Dan) has written in virtually every genre (and won recognition in many) during a career spanning seven decades. His first published poem appeared in the 1953 National High School Poetry Anthology. He edited the Oregon State College humor magazine, *Beaver dam,* and, fresh out of college, wrote a humor column, "One Man's Poison," for the *Oregon City Enterprise-Courier,* a small town daily. He laughs at himself in the mirror—and at the thugs and bumblers currently ruining things for people. He aligns with patriots striving to right the Ship of State!

About the Artist

Jim Agpalza (shown with Grok, a visitor from a distant galaxy who dropped by his Portland home one day and never left) is "a visionary and psychedelic artist," as stated on the back cover of his 2024 book, *The Art of Jim Agpalza* (Oddness, oddness.us), who "seamlessly blends art and politics in a kaleidoscopic dance of colors and ideas." No one at Road's End Press questions that fact: Consider the superb illustrations that have sprung from Jim's wild imagination onto the covers of recent Road's End Press books: *Trump Über Alles: Rhymes for Trying Times* (2022) and *The Death of Democracy* (2024).

About My Muse

My Muse—or, as I prefer, *mi Musa*—is a will o' the wisp when she so chooses, as elusive as a dapple that vanishes when I turn my head. At other times she looms like a shape-shifting wraith, lighting the path ahead, dancing playfully through my mind and heart, sifting thoughts and feelings, giving thumbs up or thumbs down with unerring accuracy, putting me on track to be the best I can be. She shares my love of truth and beauty and all things natural, and nurtures as only an Earth Mother can. I am blessed.

Glossary of Terms & Forms

Stanza examples: Three-lines, tercets; four lines, quatrains.

Rhythm and meter example: Iambic pentameter. An iamb is a rhythmical unit consisting of an unemphasized syllable followed by an emphasized syllable. Pentameter denotes five iambs in a line. Example, Page 3: "Like WAter RIsing TO the LEAVES of TREES...."

Aubade: A poem about lovers parting at dawn, dating to early medieval times. "Aubade: Dialogue at Dawn" (72)

Ballad: Often narrative in nature, first developed by 14th and 15th-century minstrels. Metered quatrains, 4-3-4-3. "The Crosscut in the Crotch" (52), "Dances with Marketeers" (96), "Flight of the Iguana" (118)

Ballade Suprême: A medieval and Renaissance form popular in France during the 13th-15th centuries. "Ballade for the Birthday of Cyrano at the Coffee Time Coffee Shop" (49)

Couplets: Rhymed *aabbcc...*: "Blue Moon" (23), "The Trickle-up Theory" (38), "'Tis the Season" (82), "Vector Control" (84), "Georgine's Abrupt Recovery" (86), "Hog Tithe" (95), "The Chair: Its Merits" (110), "Curbside Complaint" (122), "The Texas School Board Tackles Geography" (124)

Dramatic monologue: A conversation directed at a listener or reader who does not respond. "A Good Day to Die" (108)

Free verse: Unrhymed lines with no consistent metrical patterns but often structured. "Why We Love Miss America Clothed" (7), "The Moon on the Moss Beneath the Virgin" (53), "Only Mnemosyne Knows" (68), "I'm With You" (78)

Keatsian ode: Invented by John Keats. Ten-line stanzas. Combines a Sicilian quatrain, *abab,* with the Italian sestet, *cdecde.* "The Lonely Glove" (107)

Limerick: Five lines, *aabba.* Playful or absurd narrative, bouncy rhythm—two short syllables followed by a longer one. "A Trophy Fit for a King" (30), a sequence; "Three Limericks with Titles" (67), "Limerick" (83)

Narrative: Contains all the elements of a story. "The Fifteen Commandments" (41)

Nonsense verse: Absurd premise, invented words. "The Dillowy Danderhonk" (55)

Pantoum: Uses the second and fourth lines of each quatrain as the first and third lines of the next. "The Darling Buds of Barbara Bush" (32)

Sonnet: Fourteen lines, iambic pentameter.

Petrarchan/Italian—An octet (eight lines, *abbaabba*) and a sestet (six lines, *cdecde* or variation)—"Picking Blackberries" (31), four feet in place of five; "Death Came to Me Last Night' (105)

Shakesperean/English—Three quatrains and a couplet—"Willy's Wine" (34), "Rich People" (37), "The Battle of Narcissus"(43), "The Poetaster" (47), "A Guide to the Modern Sonnet" (48), "In Praise of Peter Sellers" (50), "The Curious Stares and the Hungry Eyes" (70), "I'd Rather Sail My Schooner Than Have Sex" (71), "Bronze Bosom Above Mahogany Inboard Runabout" (74), "Hangover" (104), "When Audrey Sailed" (106), "Just Deserts" (109)

Miltonic—Invented by John Milton. Free flowing, no restrictions—"Ferocious Bones" (18), "Waking Up in Willoughby" (88)

Terza rima: Three-line stanzas, *aba bcb cdc,* creating a chain-like rhythm that propels the poem. "Capillary Action" (3), "Jaw Dropping News" (20), "In Praise of Billionaires" (44)

Triplet: Three lines together, using the same end rhyme. "Birth Control" (24), "Airport Insecurity" (121)

Villanelle: Nineteen lines—five tercets followed by a quatrain. First and third lines alternately repeat in later stanzas and appear in the quatrain as the closing couplet. "Little Incubator" (81), "Willow Creek Hot Springs" (85), "The Spartans Versus the Athenians" (117)

www.ingramcontent.com/pod-product-compliance
Lightning Source LLC
Chambersburg PA
CBHW061112070526
44583CB00027B/3264